Silkworms

Written by Keith Pigdon

Series Consultant: Linda Hoyt

WorldWise™
Content-based Learning

Contents

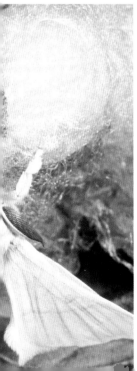

Introduction

A silkworm is not really a **worm** – it is a caterpillar.

Each caterpillar hatches from the egg of a silkworm moth. Silkworm moths are just like other moths and butterflies. They all have the same **life cycle**.

Silkworms are important to us because they make a material called silk that we use to make fabric.

Chapter 1

Growing

Eggs

The female silkworm moth lays its eggs in summer. The eggs are yellow, but they soon change to grey and stay grey through autumn and winter.

Hatching and feeding

In spring, tiny caterpillars crawl out of eggs laid by silkworm moths. These tiny caterpillars are called **larvae**. They are covered with black hair.

As soon as they hatch, the caterpillars start eating. They eat the small, fresh leaves on mulberry trees. Mulberry leaves are the only food that silkworms eat.

Like other caterpillars, silkworms spend most of their time eating. Some people think that caterpillars are eating machines because that is all they seem to do at this time of their lives.

Silkworm larvae eggs

Growing quickly

Silkworm caterpillars grow fast.

By the time they are six days old, their skins are too small for their large bodies.

They **shed** their small skins and grow larger ones. This is called **moulting**.

Over their lifetime, silkworm caterpillars moult four times. After the last moult, they grow quickly.

Chapter 2

Changing

Spinning a cocoon

In late spring, silkworm caterpillars are full of liquid silk. This liquid silk is made from the mulberry leaves they have eaten.

Now, the silkworm caterpillars stop eating.

They are ready to spin their **cocoons**, and each silkworm finds a safe place to make its cocoon.

The silkworm uses the liquid silk from inside its body to spin a cocoon. It starts by pushing out a single thread of silk from its mouth. When it is completely covered in silk, the silkworm caterpillar stops spinning.

Spinning a cocoon can take four to five days.

A silkworm cocoon

A silkworm spinning a cocoon

Did you know?

The single thread of silk that a silkworm caterpillar uses to make a cocoon can be more than one kilometre long.

Inside the cocoon

Inside the cocoon, the silkworm caterpillar **sheds** its skin and changes into a **chrysalis**.

After two or three weeks, the chrysalis becomes a moth and is ready to leave the cocoon. It uses liquid from its mouth to make a hole in the cocoon.

A silkworm moth leaving its cocoon

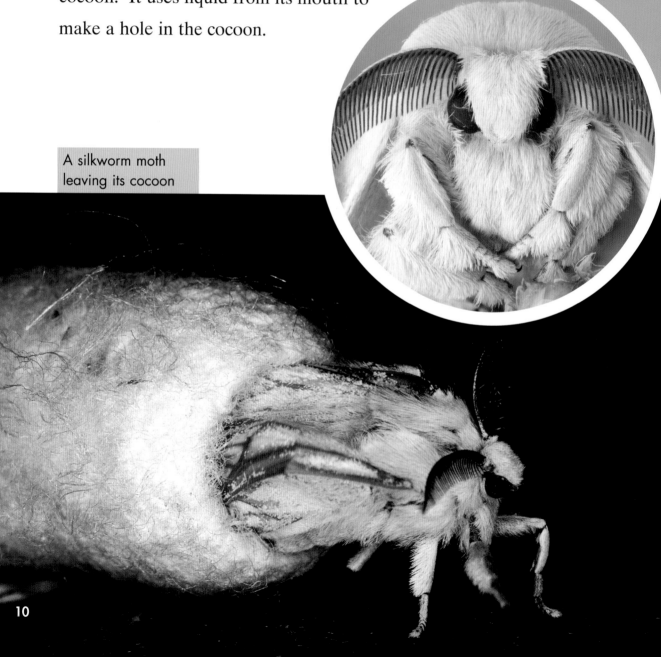

Outside the cocoon

After the silkworm moth comes out of its cocoon, it lives for only three to four days.

The adult silkworm has a wingspan of about five centimetres. The wings are cream-coloured, with dark veins, and the female is larger than the male.

The silkworm moths have small mouths, and they do not have teeth. They are moths, but they do not eat or drink.

An adult silkworm moth

Chapter 3

Mating and laying eggs

Silkworm moths cannot fly. But male silkworm moths can **flutter** around looking for a female. In spring, the moths mate by joining their tails together.

After the moths have mated, the female lays up to 500 tiny eggs. Each egg is not much bigger than a pinhead.

Each spring, the **life cycle** of the silkworm moth begins again, and tiny **larvae** hatch from the eggs.

A silkworm moth laying eggs

Silkworm moths mating

13

Life cycle of a silkworm

Eggs

Silkworm moths
mate and then
female silkworm
moths lay eggs.

Moths

Silkworm moths
come out of the
cocoons.

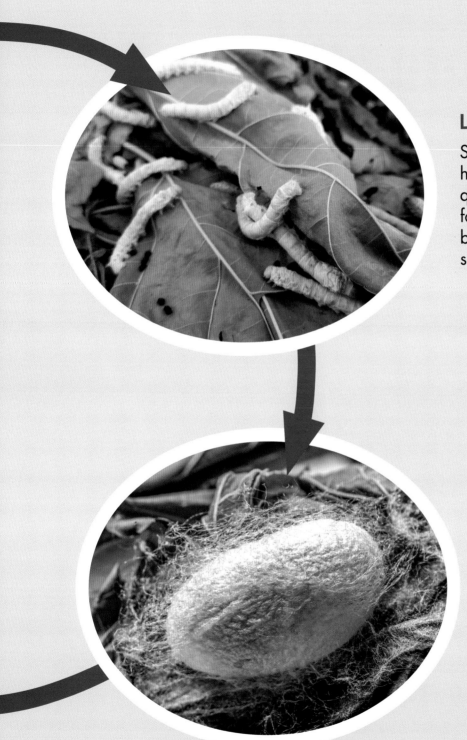

Larvae

Silkworm **larvae** hatch and grow quickly. They moult four times before they become fully grown silkworm caterpillars.

Caterpillars

Silkworm caterpillars spin **cocoons**.

Chapter 4

Making silk

A long time ago, people discovered that silkworm caterpillars produced silk. They found ways of taking the silk from the silkworm **cocoons** and making it into thread.

People took silkworms to many parts of the world. They fed them and cared for them. Over time, silkworms changed.

Making silk

Silkworms can no longer find their own food, and they depend on people to feed them. Their legs cannot grip onto leaves or branches, they cannot defend themselves against predators and silkworm moths can no longer fly. They need humans to look after them.

Find out more
What other animals can make silk?

Silkworms eat only mulberry leaves.

Conclusion

Silkworms have an interesting **life cycle** that is like other moths and caterpillars.

Silkworms have lived with humans for thousands of years. Their bodies have changed, and they now depend on humans to survive. They cannot survive in the wild.

Glossary

chrysalis   the part of its life when a silkworm caterpillar makes a case to live in as it changes into a moth

cocoon   the cover made from silk that moths make to protect themselves while they grow and change

flutter   to move wings in a fast, light motion

larvae   the young form of an insect

life cycle   the stages that all animals of the same species go through from birth to death

moulting   when a caterpillar peels off its skin and grows a bigger skin

shed   to lose skin, hair or scales

worm   an animal with a long, soft, thin body and no legs

Index